SUPERCONDUCTORS

SUPERCONDUCTORS
THE IRRESISTIBLE FUTURE

BY ALBERT STWERTKA

FRANKLIN WATTS
NEW YORK/ LONDON/TORONTO/SYDNEY
1991
A VENTURE BOOK

Photographs courtesy of: Gamma-Liaison: pp. 10 (Alain Morvan),
14 (Cindy Charles), 79 (Kaku Kurita), 80 (M. Wada);
American Institute of Physics, Niels Bohr Library: pp. 13, 48, 60;
Photo Researchers Inc./Science Photo Library: pp. 25 (Sinclair Stammers), 46
(David Parker); Francis Bitter National Magnet
Laboratory, M.I.T.: p. 43; Texas Center for Superconductivity,
University of Houston: p. 59; Fermilab: p. 71; IBM Research:
pp. 73, 83; Prof. Samuel J. Williamson, N.Y.U.: pp. 75, 76.

Library of Congress Cataloging-in-Publication Data

Stwertka, Albert.
Superconductors, the irresistible future / by Albert Stwertka.
p.   cm.—(A Venture book)
Includes bibliographical references and index.
Summary: Discusses new materials being developed to conduct energy
more efficiently and the possible impact of this development on
future technology.
ISBN 0-531-12526-2
1. Superconductors—Juvenile literature. 2. Superconductivity—
Juvenile literature. 3. Liquid helium—Electric properties—
Juvenile literature. 4. Ceramic materials—Electric properties—
Juvenile literature. [1. Superconductors. 2. Superconductivity.]
I. Title. II. Title: Superconductors.
QC611.92S78   1991
621.3—dc20   909-19309 CIP AC

CONTENTS

SUPERCONDUCTORS

1

AN IRRESISTIBLE FUTURE

In the fall of 1986 two scientists, Dr. J. George Bednorz and Dr. Karl Alexander Müller, working at the IBM research laboratories in Zurich, Switzerland, discovered a family of ceramics that became superconducting at a far higher temperature than any other known material.

Superconductivity is the ability of certain materials to carry electricity without any loss of energy. Normally, these materials become superconducting only at extremely low temperatures—often hundreds of degrees below the freezing point of water. The new ceramics, however, seemed to point the way to one of the great dreams of science: to create materials that would be superconducting at room temperatures.

Seldom has a scientific discovery led so quickly to developments that captured such wide public attention. A largely esoteric technology suddenly became a household word. Hardly a day went by without a newspaper headline announcing a new high-temperature breakthrough. Laboratories throughout the world went into a frenzy of activity as a race developed to see which one

9

J. George Bednorz (left) and Karl Alexander Müller (right) of the IBM research laboratories in Zurich, Switzerland, shared the 1987 Nobel Prize in physics for their discovery of a new class of superconducting ceramics.

could best improve and perfect the newly discovered material. Normally conservative and staid scientists started giving press releases before reporting their work to scientific journals.

SUPERCONDUCTIVITY

The phenomenon of superconductivity has always seemed magical to many scientists. It seems to violate all the laws of physics. When a substance becomes superconducting, it loses all electrical resistance. Current flows through it without losing any power. Nature seems to be offering us a "free lunch"; transmission of energy without any cost. It is the closest thing in nature to perpetual motion—an electric current that flows in a loop forever.

There was a dragon guarding this precious gift, however, a dragon in the form of a frigid barrier of superlow temperatures. Previously existing superconductors could function only if they were cooled down to just a few degrees above absolute zero, the coldest possible temperature. This extreme cold limits their use. There are at most a small number of applications that can justify the expense of cooling materials almost to the physical limit.

Bednorz and Müller slew the dragon. They not only smashed through the long-standing high-temperature record for superconductivity, but they introduced scientists to a whole new class of superconducting materials. They were awarded the Nobel Prize in physics in 1987 for their work, only one year after their discovery of high-temperature superconductivity. This marks perhaps the fastest-ever recognition of a discovery by the Nobel committee.

The explosion of superconductor research by laboratories throughout the world that followed their announcement has overwhelmed the ability of scientific journals to communicate the latest discoveries to the scientific community. Scientific meetings, not usually known for hysteria, have turned into stampedes.

When a special conference on high-temperature superconductivity was scheduled for the now famous meeting of the American Physical Society in 1987, the *New York Times* reported; "The doors opened early Wednesday evening to a roar, a blur of color and an abandonment of professorial dignity." Within three minutes, the crowd had filled all 1,200 seats, and nearly 1,000 more physicists jammed the aisles and pressed against the walls. Outside, hundreds more strained to get in. "A Woodstock of physics" is how Michael Schluter, a scientist at the Bell Laboratories of AT&T described the session at a press conference the following day. "It's a phenomenon—there's never been anything like it in the history of physics," said Dr. Ted Geballe of Stanford University. Normally staid scientists cheered and whistled as they listened to papers being presented. *Science,* the periodical of the American Association for the Advancement of Science, called it a "happening."

SHAKE AND BAKE

Equally remarkable is the ease with which these materials can be made. The elements of the new superconductors are inexpensive, and the job of mixing them relatively simple. Take the ingredients, grind them together using a mortar and pestle, and then fire them in a furnace. Scientists jokingly refer to the technique as "shake and bake." Anyone with $50 worth of chemicals and a microwave oven can make their own. Unlike most new technologies, the new *ceramic* superconductors are being used in high school classrooms only months after their discovery. Low-cost samples of the new superconducting ceramic have been available from scientific supply houses since the fall of 1987. In fact, several high school students have managed to make their own sam-

12

The "Woodstock of physics." Thousands of
physicists crammed the ballroom of the
New York Hilton in March 1987 to learn
about the latest research on high-
temperature superconducting materials.

High school students creating super-conductors. Once you have the ingredients, it is easy to make these materials in your school laboratory. A number of kits are commercially available (see p. 47).

ples. Anyone can now experiment with what has been called one of the most significant discoveries of the century.

"THRESHOLD OF A NEW AGE"

This wondrous new material promises spectacular applications. Many governments throughout the world are convinced that high-temperature superconductivity will be a major force in the future of technology, and are dedicating large amounts of money to its study. President Ronald Reagan suggested, during the start of a federal conference on superconductivity held in July of 1987, that superconductors "could bring us to the threshold of a new age."

Scientists and industrial engineers have predicted that it might be possible to save billions of dollars by using superconducting wires to transmit and store electric power. Huge magnets could levitate trains over the tracks so that they would travel without noise or friction at unheard-of speeds. Electric motors one-tenth the size of current ones could power ships and cars. There would be shoe-box-size supercomputers, advanced magnetic detecting and imaging machines for medical diagnosis, and huge superconducting magnets to initiate atomic fusion reactions. New applications are possible in ways we probably can't imagine today.

The future of high-temperature superconductors promises to be exciting. Scientists are still struggling to explain why this hard, dark ceramic has the ability to carry electric current with no loss of energy at record high temperatures. The theory of conventional superconductors cannot fully account for the properties of the new materials, and laboratories throughout the world are impatiently waiting for a new theoretical approach.

To better follow and understand this new milestone

in the history of science, we must first understand how superconductivity developed and what it has and hasn't achieved so far. The history goes back almost to the beginning of the century, and involves many of the fundamental concepts of science.

2
THE COLD FACTS

We have all experienced the sensations of hot and cold. When we drink a cup of milk, or go out of doors for a walk, or touch a piece of ice, we often use our temperature sense to describe how hot or cold it is. In general, the colder it feels, the lower the temperature.

However, judging temperature by the feel of our skin is subjective and not very accurate, and it can often be misleading. In the winter, for example, a cold block of iron will feel much colder than a block of wood at the same temperature. What is a hot shower for one person might be too cool for another. And anyone who has accidentally touched a hot frying pan knows that at even moderately extreme temperatures our temperature sense is soon replaced by pain or discomfort.

THERMOMETERS

Fortunately there are many other ways to measure temperature. One of the simplest makes use of the fact that almost everything around us responds to a change of

17

temperature by changing size. These objects get bigger when the temperature goes up, and smaller when it drops.

It is this effect of expansion and contraction that is most commonly used in thermometers. Thermometers, the thin hollow glass cylinders with their familiar glass bulb filled with mercury, are found everywhere. The expansion of the mercury tells us how to dress when going outdoors, or how much fever we have when we're ill.

To read the thermometer, of course, we use the numbers on a scale that is usually etched or printed along the side of the thermometer. The one we are all most familiar with in the United States is the Fahrenheit scale. It was devised in 1714 by Gabriel Daniel Fahrenheit, a scientific instrument maker in Amsterdam, and uses the freezing point and the boiling point of water as reference points. The temperature at which water freezes to ice is called 32°F, and the temperature at which water boils is defined as 212°F.

Another scale, the Celsius scale, is used in most parts of the world and for all scientific work. It also uses water as a reference, but the freezing point is taken as 0°C and the boiling point is 100°C. Many countries throughout the world prefer this scale for their general use as well. It was invented by Anders Celsius (1701–1744), a Swedish astronomer, and was called the "centigrade scale" until 1948, when an international conference of scientists decided that the name should be changed.

Mercury is very useful for measuring air, body, and other temperatures. At the low temperatures required for superconductivity, however, mercury is a solid, and would be of little value in a thermometer. Fortunately, scientists have other ways to measure temperature. They can make use of the decrease in the electrical resistance of most metals that occurs when the temperature falls. Another important effect uses the drop in the pressure of a gas confined in a fixed container as the temperature is lowered. Often the amount of gas that evaporates from a liquid or solid is used. Measuring the pressure of this gas, the so-called vapor pressure, will tell us the temperature.

ABSOLUTE TEMPERATURES

In the late nineteenth century scientists began to understand that there was an important relationship between temperature and energy. They found that it would be more useful to devise a temperature scale that was based on energy rather than on the physical properties of a few arbitrarily chosen substances. Mercury is used in most thermometers, but there is nothing fundamental about any of the properties of mercury. Any other liquid can be used just as well. Nor was the choice of the freezing of water as zero on the Celsius scale determined by anything but convenience.

Scientific need for a temperature scale based on energy was met by William Thompson, commonly known as Lord Kelvin, a great nineteenth-century English physicist. Lord Kelvin devised an absolute temperature scale in which zero is the coldest attainable temperature in the universe. There is no limit to how hot an object can get, but there is a limit to how cold it can get. This limit is *absolute zero.*

The best way to think about absolute zero is in terms of energy. Historically, however, Lord Kelvin devised his scale by using the fact that all gases that are heated or cooled behave in much the same way. This is because gases are so much simpler in structure than solids or liquids.

Lord Kelvin showed that if we were to draw a line on a graph indicating how the pressure of a fixed amount of gas decreases as we lower the temperature, we would find that by extending the line to a temperature of −273.15°C the gas would have a zero pressure. This is purely theoretical, of course, since all gases become liquids before this temperature is reached. But the temperature at which the pressure of any gas would become zero if it were to remain a gas is called the absolute zero of temperature. It is the coldest temperature we can ever hope to attain. Any temperature less than absolute zero is meaningless.

It's easy to see the connection between this definition of absolute temperature in terms of gas pressure and the more common one in terms of energy. We know that gases exert pressures because the molecules or atoms that make up the gas are swarming about and constantly colliding with the walls of its container. Each collision exerts a small force on the wall. Zero pressure means no collisions, which implies that there is therefore no molecular motion. Motion is energy, and we shall see in the next chapter that the energy of a system at absolute zero is close to zero.

Lord Kelvin's temperature scale, called the *Kelvin scale* (K), is the most common absolute scale and is almost universally used in scientific work. The Kelvin scale logically defines absolute zero, the coldest possible temperature, as 0 Kelvin. It then builds up the rest of the scale in degrees that are the same size as the ones on the Celsius scale. This makes going from one to the other very easy. Since we know that

$$0K = -273.15°C$$

to change a temperature expressed in degrees Kelvin to one expressed in degrees Celsius we have only to subtract 273.15 from the Kelvin temperature. For example, helium liquefies at 4.22K. To change this to degrees Celsius we simply subtract 273.15.

4.22K = (4.22 − 273.15) C = −268.83°C.

In the world of the very cold, the temperature at which some of the common gases liquefy is very important. A selection of these temperatures is shown in the table below.

USEFUL TEMPERATURES

(all measured at 1 atmosphere of pressure, i.e., the air pressure at sea level.)

Material	Temp.	
	°C	K
Helium liquefies	−268.93	4.22
Hydrogen liquefies	−252.78	20.37
Neon liquefies	−246.09	27.06
Nitrogen liquefies	−195.81	77.34
Oxygen liquefies	−182.97	90.18
Mercury freezes	−38.86	234.29
Water freezes	0.00	273.15

Although scientists can get very close, they cannot cool substances down to absolute zero exactly. The fact that absolute zero can never be attained is sometimes called the Third Law of Thermodynamics. Interestingly, no matter how low the temperature, a slight atomic vibration, representing some energy, will always be present. Scientists call this energy *zero-point energy*. The lowest temperature achieved in laboratory experiments to date is .00000003K.

3

THE ATOMIC DANCE

A lighted candle is hot enough to burn your finger, but it wouldn't be very useful as a means of heating a room in winter. A large amount of hot water flowing through pipes along the baseboard of the room, although much cooler than the flame, does a much better job.

There is obviously a difference between temperature and heat. What, then, is heat? Heat is a form of energy. The atoms making up a substance are always in motion, vibrating about randomly and colliding with each other. This motion creates heat energy. No matter if the substance is solid, liquid, or gas, the atoms are moving. That motion is more violent in a gas, less so in a liquid, and least of all in a solid.

THE FLOW OF HEAT

Our everyday experience with heat is nearly always associated with the movement of energy from one body to another. We heat up a bowl of soup on a stove burner, or heat some water in an oil-fired furnace. Heat is energy that flows from one body to another because of temperature differences. It always flows from the hot body to the cold body. When heat flows into a body, the body's internal energy increases and its temperature rises.

The temperature actually measures the average energy of the dancing atoms. The higher the temperature, the faster the atoms of a substance will move, and the faster they will dance about as they vibrate and rotate. This greater motion means that the atoms have more energy.

When heat is transferred to an object, the increase in energy it brings with it is shared by all the atoms of the object. In a large object with many atoms, the individual atoms will absorb relatively smaller shares of the added energy. The temperature increase will be less than in a smaller object with fewer atoms.

Cooling a substance slows down the atomic dance. The theoretical lower limit of temperature is the point where almost all atomic motion stops. Atoms can now line up in their most ordered arrangement, often looking like piles of cannonballs, because the arrangement is no longer disturbed by atoms jiggling back and forth. This coldest point is identical with absolute zero on the Kelvin temperature scale, which we have seen is equal to $-273.15°C$.

MAKING THINGS COLD

How do you make something colder? It's fairly easy to make something warmer. Throw some wood into the fireplace, light a fire, and a chilly room will become more comfortable. Mankind has known this for thousands of years. Cooling yourself on a hot muggy day is quite another matter. The secret of how to cool things is barely 100 years old.

One of the secrets is evaporation. Have you ever felt chilly when you stepped out of a shower? You are

*The spray from an aerosol can feels
cool because its molecules are changing
from the liquid to the gaseous state.*

being cooled by the water evaporating from your skin.
The change from water in the liquid state to water in the
gaseous state cools the liquid. The mist coming from an
aerosol can feels cool to the touch for the same reason.

We know that the average energy of the molecules
and atoms that make up a liquid is determined by its
temperature. But, in fact, some molecules have more
energy than the average, and some have less. It is the
more energetic, or faster-moving, molecules that are
most likely to escape into the gas. This leaves the less
energetic, or slower-moving, molecules behind. That's
why the liquid cools.

25

The gas also cools as it escapes and expands. This is a little more difficult to understand, but is very similar to what happens to a ball when it is thrown into the air. The ball slows down as it rises, because it is escaping from the gravitational attraction of the earth. A gas cools as it evaporates and expands because the escaping molecules or atoms are also escaping the attraction of their neighbors.

The atoms or molecules that make up a solid are usually arranged in tight patterns and packed quite close together. In a liquid, the atoms or molecules can move about more freely, but they are still closer to one another than in a gas. At short distances there is a strong force of attraction between atoms and molecules.

As the gas molecules move away from one another, the force of attraction causes them to slow down. As they slow down, the gas cools.

THE THROTTLING PROCESS

The cooling process that is used in every home refrigerator is based on a modified form of expansion. The process is one in which a liquid or gas at high pressure seeps through a tiny opening into a region of low pressure. This is called a throttling process, and the temperature drop accompanying the throttling is known as the *Joule-Thompson effect*.

The reason that a gas will cool when it is throttled is the same one that causes a liquid to cool when it evaporates. In their experiments, Joule and Thompson kept a gas at constant pressure and allowed it to flow continuously through a porous plug of tightly packed cotton into a region kept at a lower pressure. As the gas expanded, it cooled because the molecules were pulling away from each other's attractive forces.

The Joule-Thompson effect depends on the difference between the pressures in the two chambers. The

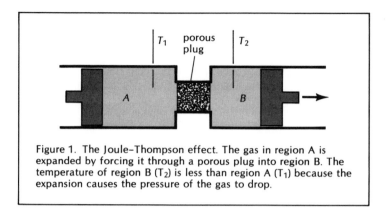

Figure 1. The Joule–Thompson effect. The gas in region A is expanded by forcing it through a porous plug into region B. The temperature of region B (T_2) is less than region A (T_1) because the expansion causes the pressure of the gas to drop.

greater the difference, the greater the drop in temperature. This fact provides a practical method for liquefying gases. In 1895 the German chemist Karl von Linde adapted the process for the large-scale liquefaction of gases.

LIQUID AIR

A sketch of a simple machine to liquefy air is shown in Figure 1. The air is first compressed and sent through the inner pipe of a double pipe called a heat exchanger. At the end of the heat exchanger the air is made to pass through a narrow opening, the throttling valve, and the pressure is reduced to normal atmospheric pressure. The Joule-Thompson expansion cools the air, which then returns through the outer pipe of the heat exchanger to the outside atmosphere. The cooled gas, as it passes in the opposite direction through the outer section of the heat exchanger, acts to cool off the incoming stream of gas that has not yet reached the throttling valve. When this cooled incoming gas undergoes throttling it starts at a lower temperature than did the gas that went through before it. Since the air always leaves the throttling valve

27

cooler than it entered, colder and colder temperatures are reached. After a few minutes, liquid air will begin to accumulate in the well.

Systems similar to this one, modified for large-scale production, were used by Karl von Linde to liquefy nitrogen and oxygen. Hydrogen was more difficult, and finally Sir James Dewar managed to do it by developing the double-walled evacuated flask to retain cold liquids. Scientists call the flask, which in popular use developed into the thermos bottle, a *Dewar flask*.

In 1895 helium, an element that had previously been known only to exist in the sun, was discovered on earth. (Helium had been discovered on the sun in 1869 when scientists observed its characteristic strong yellow line in the spectrum of the corona of the sun during an eclipse.) Helium appeared to be a "permanent" gas, an extremely unreactive gas that resisted all attempts to liquefy it. It was Heike Kamerlingh Onnes at the University of Leiden, in the Netherlands, who finally succeeded in liquefying helium on July 10, 1908. The temperature necessary to do this was just 4.22 degrees above absolute zero—4.22K. For his research into the properties of matter at extremely low temperature, including the discovery of superconductivity, Kamerlingh Onnes was awarded the Nobel Prize in physics in 1913.

Today, huge commercial plants manufacture large quantities of liquid helium, oxygen, and nitrogen, for use in scientific laboratories and industry. The cost is low: liquid nitrogen costs about as much as the same volume of milk. Liquid helium is more difficult to make and costs approximately twenty times as much as liquid nitrogen.

The lowest temperature that can be achieved fairly easily with liquid helium is about 1K. This is done by evaporation of the helium itself. A pump is used to remove the helium vapor as quickly as possible. Using special high-speed pumps, temperatures as low as 0.7K have been achieved.

MAGNETIC COOLING

Still lower temperatures depend on the magnetic properties of a group of crystals called *paramagnetic salts*. In 1926 Peter Debye in Germany and William Giaque in America simultaneously suggested using these magnetic properties to attain temperatures below 1K.

Certain elements like *gadolinium,* iron, chromium, and cerium, behave like little magnets when they interact chemically with other elements to form a crystal. The gadolinium jiggles about in the crystal with the usual thermal energy, so that the little magnets orient themselves in more or less random positions.

To achieve temperatures in the millikelvin (thousandths of a Kelvin) range, the gadolinium compound is placed in a glass tube and cooled to a temperature of about 1K by means of a liquid helium bath. The entire assembly is then placed between the poles of an electromagnet. The current in the electromagnet is slowly increased, increasing its magnetic field. The individual gadolinium ions begin to align themselves with this field, behaving very much like compass needles lining up with the earth's magnetic field.

The alignment of billions of little magnets that were formerly pointing every which way magnetizes the salt. The heat given off during this process is absorbed by the liquid helium, some of which evaporates. When the salt is as magnetized as it can be, and as cold as liquid helium can make it, the electromagnet is rolled away. The salt, which is now isolated from everything by a vacuum, begins to demagnetize itself and in the process cools, just as a liquid cools when a vapor is drawn away from it.

LOW-TEMPERATURE MEASUREMENTS

You might wonder how we measure temperatures this low. Often a helium-gas thermometer is used. The pres-

29

sure of a sample of helium gas kept at constant volume will increase with increasing temperature. The same is true of any gas. An automobile tire, for example, has a higher pressure after a long drive because the tire gets hot. With proper calibration, a pressure measurement using the gas thermometer can easily be translated into a temperature.

Another useful means of temperature measurement takes advantage of the change in electrical resistance of a conductor with temperature. This is true even for conductors that are not metals. In actual practice, the most common material used is a carbon resistor, of the kind commonly found in hi-fi receivers and television sets. The resistance can be measured with a device called an ohmmeter.

Liquid helium is important in superconductivity work, and measuring its temperature is therefore important. A common way scientists use to measure the temperature of a sample of liquid helium is to determine its vapor pressure. You will remember that the gas that collects over a liquid is called a vapor. This vapor exerts a pressure, just like any other gas. It is called the vapor pressure. The value of the vapor pressure depends only on the temperature. As you decrease the temperature, the vapor pressure decreases.

As we shall see in the next chapter, the production of liquid helium and the ability to measure its temperature was the key to the era of ultra-low-temperature science.

4

AMAZING HELIUM

The ability to liquefy helium was crucial for further progress in the world of the supercold. Experimental environments could now be kept cold for long periods of time by either surrounding them with or immersing them in baths of liquid helium. Scientists and engineers could for the first time explore how various materials behaved at temperatures close to absolute zero. One of the first things they found in this strange new world was that liquid helium was interesting in its own right.

After Kamerlingh Onnes had succeeded in liquefying helium, he went on to what seemed to him the next frontier in low-temperature work, to turn helium into a solid. He tried with every means at his command to lower the temperature as far as he could. Liquid helium was first cooled by allowing it to evaporate, and then his most powerful vacuum pumps were applied to cool the liquid still further by drawing off more helium vapor. He reached temperatures of approximately 1K, but the helium still remained a liquid. Kamerlingh Onnes never succeeded in solidifying helium, and the reason remained a mystery to him.

Scientists know today that Kamerlingh Onnes was engaged in a hopeless task. It is impossible to turn liquid helium into a solid at ordinary pressures. Scientists have recently managed to make solid helium, but only at very high pressures. Pressures some thirty times normal atmospheric pressure are needed at about 1K to do the job.

To understand why helium will not become a solid except at very high pressures we have to make use of one of the important principles of modern physics. Scientists have discovered that when a system of atoms is confined in a given space, it is impossible for the atoms to have zero energy. The reason for this is complicated and has to do with the uncertainties that seem to dominate the atomic world. In effect, scientists now know that the more precisely we can define the position of atoms, the less we know about their energy.

As mentioned earlier, this minimum energy of atoms—that is, the energy that atoms can never rid themselves of—is known as zero-point energy. Because of zero-point energy, atoms are always jiggling about or vibrating in some fashion. There is always some motion no matter how low we make the temperature. And it is this motion that prevents helium from freezing. In a solid, you will remember, the atoms are held together in a fairly rigid pattern, so that very little motion is possible. The zero-point energy is sufficiently strong to prevent the light helium atoms from sticking together to form a solid.

SUPERFLUIDS

One of the most interesting properties of liquid helium, and the property that gives it the name *superfluid,* is its *viscosity.* The viscosity of a liquid is a measure of how easily the liquid flows; that is, it measures how "sticky" it is. The more difficult it is to get a liquid to flow, the greater the viscosity. Viscosity can be thought of as a kind of friction, an internal friction that prevents various parts of the liquid from sliding easily by each other. Honey and molasses are examples of two very common liquids that have a high viscosity. Water, on the other hand, has a much lower viscosity; it flows more easily.

Ordinary liquid helium near its boiling point at 4.2K behaves more or less like a normal liquid. An extraordinary change occurs, however, as it is cooled below 2.17K. One finds that it loses all viscosity. Normally, if you try to make a liquid flow through a narrow tube (called a capillary tube) you have to exert some pressure to keep it going. Liquid helium, below 2.17K, flows through the finest tubes without any outside force being required. If liquid helium is placed in a ceramic dish, for example, and cooled below 2.17K, it pours through the bottom of the dish as if flowing through a fine mesh.

The change in liquid helium is so dramatic at a temperature of 2.17K, that it is known as *helium I* above this temperature, and *helium II* below it. The changeover point is called the *lambda point*. It is not only the flow through a narrow orifice that is so extraordinary, but helium in its superfluid state will flow along any surface with absolutely no friction whatsoever.

An astonishing example of this is a half-filled flask of helium II that will actually empty itself without any outside help (Figure 2). An empty flask is first lowered into a bath of helium II and partially filled. When the flask is lifted straight out, and suspended in an upright position, a film of helium starts to climb up the wall of the flask, pulled up by the attractive force of the wall of the flask. It is a similar force that causes ordinary water to form a slightly curved upper surface inside a glass.

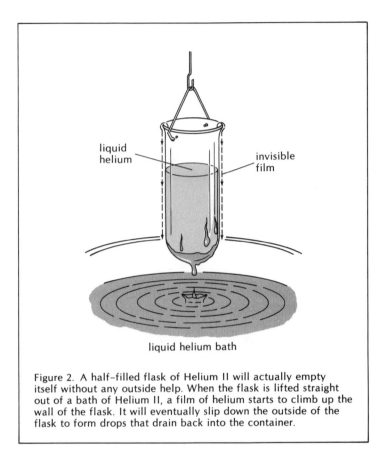

liquid helium

invisible film

liquid helium bath

Figure 2. A half-filled flask of Helium II will actually empty itself without any outside help. When the flask is lifted straight out of a bath of Helium II, a film of helium starts to climb up the wall of the flask. It will eventually slip down the outside of the flask to form drops that drain back into the container.

The film of helium, however, flowing without any loss of energy due to viscosity, will keep flowing up and eventually slip down the outside of the flask to form drops that drain right back into the surrounding container. This process continues until the flask is empty.

CONDUCTOR OF HEAT

Scientists have also found that helium II is an excellent conductor of heat. As liquid helium is cooled below the lambda point, its ability to conduct heat increases by a factor of over a million. Astonishingly, its heat-conducting efficiency is hundreds of times greater than most metals'. An example of this is the behavior of liquid helium when it is made to boil at low temperatures.

It is difficult to imagine any material near absolute zero boiling, but liquid helium can be made to boil by reducing the pressure above it. When boiling, liquid helium looks like any other liquid, with bubbles forming throughout the liquid and rising rapidly to the surface. As the liquid helium is cooled and passes through the lambda point, however, bubbling stops and the liquid becomes very quiet. The reason for the sudden change is the dramatic increase in the conductivity of heat. Energy is now distributed so quickly throughout the liquid that evaporation occurs only at the surface. No pockets of helium vapor form in the interior of the helium, and there is therefore no bubbling or agitation of any kind except at the surface.

Unlike any other known liquid, helium II actually flows toward a heat source. One of the earliest experiments demonstrating this reverse flow, is shown in Figure 3. A U-tube packed with fine emery powder is connected to a hollow tube and immersed in a pool of helium II. The system looks somewhat like an inverted cane. Although the U-tube is sealed at both ends with cotton wool, the helium II can flow freely through the powder and cotton plugs into the tube. If a beam of light is now made to shine on the powder, heat is absorbed, and a strong flow of helium II from the pool toward the heated U-tube is produced. The flow can be so violent at times that a jet of helium can be forced up through the vertical tube to heights of 10 inches (25 cm). This phenomenon, known as the "fountain" effect, occurs because helium II is changed into ordinary helium by the heat and undergoes an enormous increase in viscosity. The helium now is too sticky to flow back down through

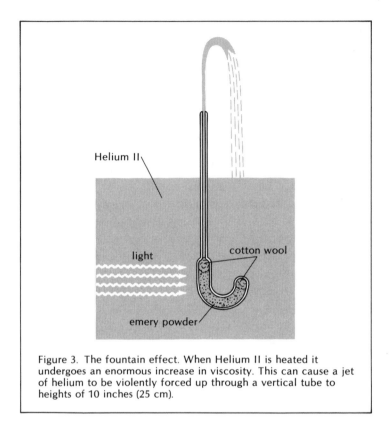

Figure 3. The fountain effect. When Helium II is heated it undergoes an enormous increase in viscosity. This can cause a jet of helium to be violently forced up through a vertical tube to heights of 10 inches (25 cm).

the emery powder, and is pushed from behind by helium in the superfluid state flowing in.

The most important effect uncovered by the super-cooling powers of liquid helium, however, was that of superconductivity. It was the great Dutch scientist Kamerlingh Onnes, working in his laboratory in Leiden, who first observed the sudden disappearance of all electrical resistance in certain metals at temperatures close to absolute zero. In the next chapter we shall take a closer look at this phenomenon and explore how it led scientists to a more profound understanding of matter.

5

SUPERCONDUCTIVITY

One of the most exciting chapters in the history of science began in 1908, when Heike Kamerlingh Onnes succeeded in liquefying helium. He now had the ability to achieve and maintain temperatures of several degrees above absolute zero. Kamerlingh Onnes and his assistants quickly set to work investigating the various properties of matter at these incredibly low temperatures. One of the properties that Kamerlingh Onnes investigated was the ability of metals to conduct electricity at low temperatures.

THE WANDERING ELECTRON

Our understanding of electricity is firmly based on the pioneering work of J. J. Thompson, a physics professor at England's Cambridge University. It was Thompson who showed that one of the fundamental particles that make up an atom, the electron, can detach itself from its parent atom and have an independent existence.

Normally atoms are electrically neutral; that is, they have exactly the same number of positive and negative charges. When the electron, which has a negative charge, detaches itself from an atom, it unbalances this equality of charges. It leaves behind an atom that is now positively charged. This positively charged remainder is called an *ion.*

It soon became clear that the flow of electric current in a metal could be traced to the motion of free electrons within the metal. Some of the electrons around the atoms that make up a metal are very loosely bound. They can easily detach themselves from their parent atom, and are more or less free to wander through the metal.

Some scientists like to think of a metal wire as a box holding a "gas" of free electrons. When the wire is attached to a generator or other pressure source, these electrons are made to drift through the wire to produce what we call an electric current.

In a nonconductor of electricity such as wood, the electrons are not free but are tightly bound to their parent atoms.

If you could use a supermicroscope to look at the metal conductor, you would see the free electrons moving through a large open framework of ions neatly arranged in repeating patterns. This framework, called a "lattice," is fairly rigid so that the ions are not free to move very far from their fixed positions.

At ordinary temperatures, you would notice that neither the electron "gas" nor the ions are at rest. The free electrons are moving about rapidly in random directions, and the ions are jiggling about their fixed position in the lattice. These random motions make up what scientists call thermal energy. If you were to decrease the temperature, the motion would become less agitated.

38

ELECTRIC CURRENT

If the two ends of a metal-wire conductor are now connected to a battery at normal temperatures, an electric pressure appears within the wire. The free electrons respond to this pressure, as does any object when pushed, by accelerating in the direction of the pressure. If the metal consisted of nothing but electrons, the electrons would move faster and faster. In a real metal, however, as the electrons begin to pick up speed, they collide with the ions that make up the lattice. When they bump into one of the ions making up the lattice they bounce in various random directions, so that their directed motion under the influence of the force is disturbed. And every time they bounce they can lose much of their speed, even momentarily coming to a dead stop.

ELECTRICAL RESISTANCE

The energy lost by the electron during such a collision is transferred to the lattice as heat. This is why electric heaters and light bulbs work. In the transmission of electricity, however, this heating effect is undesirable. For example, some 20 percent of the energy sent through high-tension lines is lost in the form of heat generated as the current encounters resistance in the copper wire. If the current flow is to be maintained, the energy source must reaccelerate the electrons after each collision.

The general effect produced by these many electron collisions is called *electrical resistance*. The behavior of the electron is roughly analogous to a car driving in city traffic. It constantly is accelerating and stopping for traffic lights. Much of the energy consumed in using gasoline is lost to heating the brake pads and tires. Although the car never really travels very fast, it does eventually "drift" from one street to another.

The production of heat as the electrons drift through the wire is fine if you are interested in toasting some bread. If, on the other hand, you are interested in transmitting as much energy as possible from a hydroelectric plant to your home, the loss of useful electric energy in the form of heat can be very expensive.

To reduce the electrical resistance, then, one should look for ways of reducing the collisions the electrons make with the lattice. One way of doing this is to lower the temperature. Lowering the temperature reduces the thermal motion of the ions that make up the lattice. As the amplitude of their vibrations gets smaller, the chance that a drifting electron will collide with an ion also gets smaller.

VANISHING RESISTANCE

It was this drop in resistance with temperature that Kamerlingh Onnes was studying. During April of 1911, just three years after he had succeeded in liquefying helium, he was performing a series of conduction experiments with mercury. Mercury was an ideal substance to investigate since it could easily be purified by distillation. Scientists always have to be careful about the effect of impurities, even in tiny trace amounts, on the electrical resistance of ordinary metals.

Much to his amazement, the electrical resistance of mercury, a solid at liquid-helium temperatures, did not just decrease but completely vanished at 4.15K. It became a perfect conductor. Kamerlingh Onnes later coined the word "superconductivity" to explain this previously unknown phenomenon. Even now, some eighty years after the discovery, it still seems hard to believe in this form of "perpetual motion." There was no doubt that it existed, however, and a year later he and a colleague showed that tin became superconducting below a temperature of 3.7K, and lead became superconducting below a temperature of 7.2K. The temperature at which these metals become superconducting was called the *critical temperature, T(c)*.

The critical temperatures of some common elemental metals are shown in Table 1. These elements are classified as *type I superconductors*. It is interesting to note that while copper, silver, and gold are all good conductors of electricity at normal temperatures, they cannot be made superconducting.

TABLE 1. CRITICAL TEMPERATURES OF TYPE II SUPERCONDUCTORS

Superconductor	*Critical Temperature (K)*
Mercury (Hg)	4.153
Lead (Pb)	7.193
Aluminum (A1)	1.196
Tin (Sn)	3.722
Tungsten (W)	0.015
Zinc (Zn)	0.85
Titanium (Ti)	0.39

The resistance of a superconductor is truly zero. By the beginning of World War I, Kamerlingh Onnes and his group had shown that electric currents induced in superconductors would persist and circulate for long periods of time after the original energy source was removed from the circuit. These persistent currents are called *supercurrents*. In one experiment conducted in England in 1956, a persistent current was maintained in a superconducting ring for two and a half years. The experiment had to be stopped because of a trucking strike that halted the supply of liquid helium.

CRITICAL MAGNETIC FIELDS

Whatever hopes Kamerlingh Onnes had for any practical application of his discovery were soon dampened by the strange behavior of some of his superconductors in a magnetic field. He discovered that the critical temperature at which such elements as mercury, tin, and lead become superconducting decreases when the metal is placed in a magnetic field. The stronger the magnetic field, the lower the critical temperature. To make matters worse, when the magnetic field is increased to a certain critical value, called the *critical magnetic field, B(c),* superconductivity completely disappears. Mercury, for example, has a critical magnetic field of 0.041 Teslas, while that of lead is 0.080 Teslas. (The Tesla is a common unit used to measure the strength of magnetic fields.) For comparison, the earth's magnetic field, which pulls the needle of a compass, is approximately 0.00005 Teslas.

The magnetic effect was very discouraging because it is impossible to avoid magnetic fields. One of the most important effects of any electric current is that it creates a magnetic field around any conductor through which it passes. This has been known since 1819, when the Danish scientist Hans Christian Oersted discovered that a compass needle was deflected by a current-carrying wire. Current flowing through a superconductor will, therefore, inevitably create a magnetic field. The stronger the current, the greater the created field and the lower the critical temperature. If the current is high enough, it can create a magnetic field strong enough to destroy its own superconducting state. The current that will eliminate superconductivity is called the critical current.

It was always hoped that superconductors could be used to make powerful and efficient electromagnets. Electromagnets are present everywhere in our daily life. They make use of the magnetic field generated when an electric current is passed through a conductor.

Such magnets are essential features of doorbells, television picture tubes, particle accelerators for nuclear

This superconducting solenoid is used in a powerful magnet system developed by the National Magnet Laboratory at the Massachusetts Institute of Technology.

research, and the cranes that lift automobiles at junk-yards. One of the most powerful magnets at the National Magnet Laboratory produces a field of 23 Teslas, and uses as much electricity as is generated by a small power station. Obviously, mercury, aluminum, and tin have critical fields that are far too low to permit using them to fabricate such powerful electromagnets. This is true for all the type-I elemental superconductors.

TYPE II SUPERCONDUCTORS

During the 1950s and 1960s the search for supercon-ductors with higher transition (critical) temperatures intensified. A host of new materials was discovered, many of them exotic alloys of the element niobium, whose chemical symbol is Nb.

Transition temperatures and critical magnetic fields slowly crept up. By 1973, the niobium-germanium alloy Nb_3Ge was found to be superconducting at a temperature of 23.2K, a record high that lasted until 1986. The critical field of Nb_3Ge was 38 Teslas, high enough to consider using the alloy for electromagnets. The largest superconducting magnets now used in particle accelerators produce fields of about 6.5 Teslas. The intermetallic superconductors are known as *type II superconductors.* Some critical temperature and critical field values of type II superconductors are shown in Table 2. The magnetic field associated with a strong electromagnet rarely exceeds 2 Teslas. This means that an enormous magnet wound with Nb_3Al could be constructed, since it could sustain fields of 32.4 Teslas and still be superconducting. Unfortunately, maintaining it at its critical temperature of 18.7K would be difficult and expensive.

MEISSNER EFFECT

The magnetic properties of superconductors are as mysterious and unique as its electrical ones. In 1933 two early pioneers in the field, Walther Hans Meissner and his colleague Robert Ochsenfeld, found that when type I superconductors are cooled below their critical temperatures they not only lose all electrical resistance but they also lose all interior magnetic fields. Any field that might have been present before the metals became superconducting is gone.

There are magnetic fields everywhere around us. There is the earth's magnetic field, as well as all the fields generated by the electrical machinery and electronic devices we use in our everyday life. These invis-

44

TABLE 2. CRITICAL TEMPERATURES AND CRITICAL FIELDS OF SOME TYPE II SUPERCONDUCTORS

Super-conductor	Critical Temp-erature (K)	Critical Field (Teslas)
Nb_3Sn	18.0	24.5
Nb_3Al	18.7	32.4
KNb_3Ge	23.2	38
NbTi	10	15
Nb_3Ga	20	35

ible fields pass right through us and all the objects around us. But superconductors push these fields aside and expel them from their interiors.

The expulsion of all magnetic fields from the interior of a superconductor is known as the *Meissner effect*. It is as important in defining type I superconductors as is the loss of all electrical resistance. A superconductor shields its interior from magnetic fields by setting surface currents that act as a mirror, reflecting any external field away from its interior. The magnetic field produced by the surface currents exactly cancels the external field inside the substance and opposes it outside. These surface currents can flow without any energy loss and so can last as long as the magnetic field is present.

Bring the north pole of a bar magnet near a super-conductor and the surface currents will make the super-conductor behave like a north pole, too. Since north poles repel one another, the superconductors will push the bar magnet away. The most dazzling demonstration of the Meissner effect is the floating of a small permanent magnet above a superconductor. The phenomenon of magnetic levitation has raised the possibility of magnet-ically levitated trains gliding over a track without friction or noise.

A magnet floats freely above one of the new high-temperature yttrium-barium-copper oxide superconductors. This phenomenon is due to the Meissner effect, the expulsion of all magnetic fields from the interior of a superconductor. The glowing vapor is liquid nitrogen, which cools the supercon- ductor to the necessary temperature.

DO-IT-YOURSELF KITS

A number of do-it-yourself kits that demonstrate the principles of superconductivity are on the market. Here are just two of them:

* A superconductivity demonstration kit and superconducting disk-fabrication kit can be purchased from Superconductive Components, Inc., 1145 Chesapeake Ave., Columbus, OH 43212.

* A superconducting pellet (cat. no. A37,446) and a high-quality samarium-cobalt magnet (cat. no. A37,447) can be obtained from Edmund Scientific Co., 101 E. Gloucester Pike, Barrington, NJ 08007. These demonstrate magnetic levitation quite nicely. You will need some liquid nitrogen for this experiment (**Caution!**), which can be purchased from a local supplier.

THE BCS THEORY

It took more than forty years for scientists to explain why some materials become superconducting at low temperatures. Presented in 1957 by John Bardeen, Leon Cooper, and J. Robert Schrieffer, the explanation is known as the *BCS theory* for the initials of its authors, who shared the 1972 Nobel Prize in physics for their effort.

The central idea of the BCS theory is that in a superconductor it is not single electrons that carry the current but pairs of electrons. Somehow, pairs of electrons experience an attractive force and drift through the conductor coupled together in what scientists call a *Cooper pair.*

*John Bardeen (left), Leon Cooper (center),
and J. Robert Schrieffer (right) postulated
that pairs of electrons (rather than single
electrons) carry the current in low-temperature
superconductors. They received the Nobel
Prize for physics in 1972 for this breakthrough in superconductivity theory.*

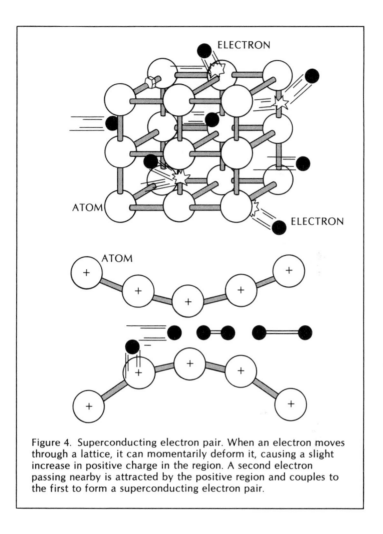

Figure 4. Superconducting electron pair. When an electron moves through a lattice, it can momentarily deform it, causing a slight increase in positive charge in the region. A second electron passing nearby is attracted by the positive region and couples to the first to form a superconducting electron pair.

But two electrons have like charges and normally repel one another. Where does the attraction come from? The answer is that it comes from the ions that make up the metal lattice through which the electrons are moving. When an electron passes through the lattice, it can momentarily deform the lattice. Since the lattice consists of positive ions, the deformation results in a slight in-

49

crease in the concentration of positive charge in this region (Figure 4).

But the ions are much heavier than the electrons and therefore more sluggish and slow-moving, so that the deformation persists for some time. A second electron passing nearby later, before the positive ions have had a chance to return to their normal positions, is attracted to this positive region. The net result is that the second electron is paired to the first to form a superconducting electron pair. The electrons move in tandem like surfers being carried to shore by the same wave. It is the interaction of the lattice that supplies the force of attraction between the pairs.

This would explain the rather puzzling fact that copper or silver, both excellent conductors at room temperature, cannot be made superconducting. The reason they are good conductors is just because there is not a strong interaction between their electrons and the lattice. It is, after all, the lattice interactions that couple the electrons in a superconductor.

The pairing of electrons has been compared by John Bardeen, now a professor emeritus at the University of Illinois, to a phase change, similar to the change of phase when water turns into steam or ice. "What causes a material to become superconducting is a phase change," he says. "You can think of it as electrons condensing into a new state." The electrons condense into a new state consisting of Cooper pairs.

In this new state, the electron pairs act collectively rather than independently. When paired together they avoid the usual collisions with impurities and ions that cause resistance and dissipate energy in the form of heat. The pairs behave like a single system so that you can't change the speed of any one pair without changing the speed of all other pairs at the same time. It is an all-or-nothing situation. This behavior has been compared to a

50

group of mountain climbers tied to one another with ropes. If any one of them were to fall into a crevasse, the others would immediately pull him out.

This pairing mechanism seemed adequate to explain superconductivity in every material until Bednorz and Müller appeared on the scene in 1986.

6

HIGH-TEMPERATURE SUPERCONDUCTIVITY: THE BARRIERS

Much of the research in superconductivity since its discovery some seventy-five years ago has been devoted to finding new superconducting materials (Figure 5). It was hoped that these new materials would have higher critical temperatures and could be used in a practical temperature range. Progress was discouragingly slow. For a decade, 23K, the critical temperature of one of the niobium alloys, stood as the high-temperature barrier.

This barrier had to be broken if all the wonderful technological innovations associated with superconductivity were to be brought into the range of the practical. No progress was really possible if almost all activity was to be limited to a small number of highly specialized laboratories that had the ability to work within a few degrees of absolute zero. Liquid helium is needed to produce the frigid temperatures for many of these applications, and liquid helium is expensive—about $10 to $15 a gallon. It also requires a complex refrigeration system.

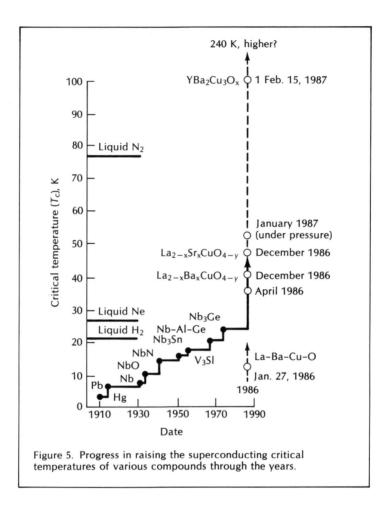

Figure 5. Progress in raising the superconducting critical temperatures of various compounds through the years.

The goal of many laboratories became to find a material that would become superconducting above the temperature at which nitrogen liquefies. The liquid nitrogen "barrier," the temperature at which this common gas becomes liquid, is 77K. Still cold, but a major step above helium. At this temperature superconductivity would begin to approach a range where practical applications were possible. Since nitrogen makes up about 80

54

percent of ordinary air, using nitrogen is almost equivalent to using air. Liquid nitrogen is cheap, about 25¢ a gallon. It is relatively long-lasting and so easy to work with that scientists carry it around in ordinary Thermos bottles.

Still better, of course, would be a material whose transition temperature was above 195K, the temperature of dry ice. And if the barrier could be pushed up another 100K it would mean the final realization of a room-temperature superconductor.

BREAKING THE NIOBIUM BARRIER

The new era in superconductivity began in 1986, when Johannes Georg Bednorz and Karl Alexander Müller, working at the IBM Research Laboratories in Zurich, Switzerland, discovered the superconducting properties of a compound of barium, lanthanum, copper, and oxygen. This oxide had a transition temperature of 35K, a temperature much higher than BCS theory would have predicted. The niobium barrier (niobium was until then the substance with the highest transition temperature) had been broken. The discovery restored the confidence of scientists that much higher critical temperature values could be achieved.

It is a remarkable achievement that has galvanized the entire scientific community, spurred a global race for industrial and military applications, and led two scientists to a Nobel Prize. Now, less than two years after the landmark discovery, even high school students can demonstrate high-temperature superconductivity for less than $50.

Müller had become interested in superconductivity while on a sabbatical visit to the United States in 1978. His decision to study ceramic oxides as a possible superconductor was most unusual. Ceramics are generally known as insulators and are notoriously poor conductors of electricity at room temperatures. Of particular interest to him were a class of ceramics called *perovskites*. These ceramics, which are chemical compounds that contain oxygen combined with metal elements, are called metallic oxides. The atomic arrangement of these elements in a perovskite crystal always takes a definite and characteristic form.

The conventional wisdom of the scientific community was very much against the choice of oxides as candidates for superconductivity. For Müller, however, the choice was not as farfetched as one might think. For one thing, the investigation of oxide materials had a long tradition in the Zurich research labs. For another, two French scientists at the University of Caen had recently found traces of electrical conduction in a new ceramic compound they created of copper, oxygen, lanthanum, and barium. They, unfortunately, never thought of testing it for superconductivity.

A CONDUCTING CERAMIC

There were also hints from the theoretical work of other scientists. Müller was certainly aware of the very successful BCS theory. This theory, you will remember, explained superconductivity in terms of bound electron pairs that were formed by an interaction with the metal lattice. Just such an interaction between electrons and lattice had been predicted in certain metallic oxides by what is known as the *Jahn-Teller effect*. This theory is named for Herman A. Jahn of the University of Hampton in England and Edward Teller of Lawrence Livermore Laboratory in California—the same Teller noted for his work on the hydrogen bomb.

There were many such clues, but chiefly it was scientific intuition and many years of working by trial and error that led Müller and Bednorz to the discovery of a superconducting metallic oxide. Their work was so bizarre that they even kept it a secret from their superiors at IBM.

The oxide that Müller and Bednorz finally manufactured looked nothing like a conductor of electricity. It was a black ceramic material that had been fabricated by *sintering* together some of the elements. Sintering is the scientific name for combining elements in powder form to form a solid by subjecting them to high temperatures and pressures. To complicate matters, they found that the ability of their oxide to become superconducting was very sensitive to the temperatures at which the sintering and subsequent cooling took place.

In September 1986 Müller and Bednorz published their findings in the German journal *Zeitschrift für Physik*. It took some time before news of the breakthrough spread through the scientific community. No announcement was made, and even their colleagues at IBM were kept in the dark to delay the pressure of competition. Bednorz is reported as saying that by not calling attention to their work, they could continue in peace for a year or two. "They scooped the world," said Philip Anderson, a Nobel laureate physicist from Princeton University. "They managed to get it published and people still didn't pay any attention to it."

As scientists finally began to learn of the experiment, the first reaction was skepticism. The large increase in the critical temperature seemed too good to be true, and the material used seemed too exotic.

It was a team of scientists headed by Shoji Tanaka at the University of Tokyo that first took the report seriously. They repeated the experiment and confirmed the results. This was quickly followed by a group in China. Then, as Müller said, "the United States sat up." Large industrial laboratories like Bell Labs, the chief research facility of A.T.&T., began to manufacture similar materials. At the University of Houston in Texas, a group headed by Paul C. W. Chu attempted not only to confirm but to improve the original results obtained in Zurich. Soon, scientists from the University of Alabama were involved.

A branch of physics that had been slowly plodding along for decades suddenly became the hottest topic in all of science. The race was on. Who could get to the boiling point of nitrogen first? On February 16, 1987, the National Science Foundation, which supported Chu and other scientists, announced that Paul C. W. Chu of the University of Houston and Maw-Kuen Wu of the University of Alabama had observed a critical temperature as high as 93K in a new compound they had created. They had broken through the barrier.

1-2-3 SUPERCONDUCTOR

The new material was an oxide of barium, copper, and the rare-earth element yttrium. Chu had actually measured a true Meissner effect in the material on January 12. This test is as crucial in establishing true superconductivity as the lack of electrical resistance. He also filed a patent application on the same day. The composition of his new material was finally disclosed in the March 2 issue of *Physical Review Letters.* This famous paper begins, "A stable and reproducible superconductivity between 80K and 92K has been unambiguously observed both resistively and magnetically in a new Y-Ba-Cu-O compound at ambient pressure."

Paul C. W. Chu of the University of Houston led the team of researchers that created the 1-2-3 ($YBa_2 Cu_3 O_7$) superconductor, which broke all previous high-temperature superconductivity records.

Scientist Robert Cava of Bell Labs holds a disk and tape made from the new high-temperature superconducting ceramic materials.

The chemical formula of this magic material has the approximate composition $YBa_2Cu_3O_7$. It has come to be known as the 1-2-3 compound for its relative atomic proportions of yttrium, barium, and copper. It is the rare-earth element yttrium that is the most unfamiliar. The so-called *rare earths* are a group of seventeen elements that are called rare because they were first found in rare minerals. Despite their name, rare earths are relatively abundant in the earth's crust. According to geologists, vast amounts would be accessible if demand increased. The rare earth yttrium, for example, is thought to be more abundant than lead.

Chu was led to this compound by a fascinating

group of experiments. The University of Houston has quite an extensive laboratory for testing materials at very high pressure. Chu wondered what would happen to one of these superconducting oxides if it were subjected to high pressures. He found that the critical temperatures began to rise as he increased the pressure. Chu reasoned that the pressure was decreasing the effective size of atoms. If squashing the atoms of the oxide somehow increased transition temperatures, perhaps squeezing them from inside could do the same thing. Smaller atoms appeared to give higher transition temperatures, so he began to substitute smaller atoms into the oxide.

Physicists at Bell Laboratories had reported a transition temperature of 40K when strontium was substituted for barium. Strontium is similar to barium but has a smaller atomic structure. A major race was developing between laboratories, and they began feverishly to change recipes by substituting a host of similar metals of different sizes into their oxides.

The breakthrough came when Chu substituted yttrium for lanthanum. Yttrium has the same chemical properties as lanthanum, but is smaller. Maw-Kuen Wu, a former graduate student of Chu's, and leader of a team of researchers at the University of Alabama also working on the compound, recalls "We were so excited and nervous that our hands were shaking. At first we were suspicious that it was an error." Within a week of the announcement, a host of other laboratories had reproduced the results.

With the right recipe and materials, the 1-2-3 compound is relatively easy to make. Scientists often say that all one has to do is "shake and bake." A chemist can make a batch in a matter of hours. Mix some finely powdered oxides of copper, barium, and yttrium in the proportion of one part yttrium to two parts barium to three parts copper. Bake the mixture in an oven at about 950°C (1,742°F) for six hours. Cool the mixture rapidly, regrind it, and reheat it. Then cool it slowly in the oven to 450°C (842°F) in the presence of oxygen. Remove it from the oven, and you're ready to go.

THE YTTRIUM BREAKTHROUGH

The next question to answer, of course, is why are these oxides superconducting. After just two months of research, and an amazing total of some fifty papers from laboratories in a dozen countries, the structure of the 1-2-3 oxide emerged. It strongly resembled the structure of a perovskite, the mineral that had intrigued Müller.

The structure of an ideal perovskite crystal is difficult to visualize. It is a three-dimensional structure filled with what seems to be a jumble of different atoms. But there is, in fact, a pattern. Visualized as simply as possible, it can be thought of as three cubes piled on one another. There is a barium atom in the center of the top and bottom cubes, and an yttrium atom in the center of the middle cube. There are copper atoms at the corners. Each yttrium atom is surrounded by eight oxygen atoms, and each barium atom by ten oxygen atoms (see Figure 6). To complicate matters, the structure is an imperfect perovskite structure in that there seem to be some oxygen atoms missing.

Scientists feel that it is these vacant sites that are crucial to superconductivity. In the crystal itself, the missing oxygen atoms seem to produce a layered structure. They also seem to produce long chains of copper and oxygen atoms. It is these features that many theorists think is central to the phenomenon of superconductivity.

CHAINS AND FLAWS

The present highly successful theory of superconductivity, the BCS theory, seems to break down when it comes to explaining high-temperature superconductivity. Sci-

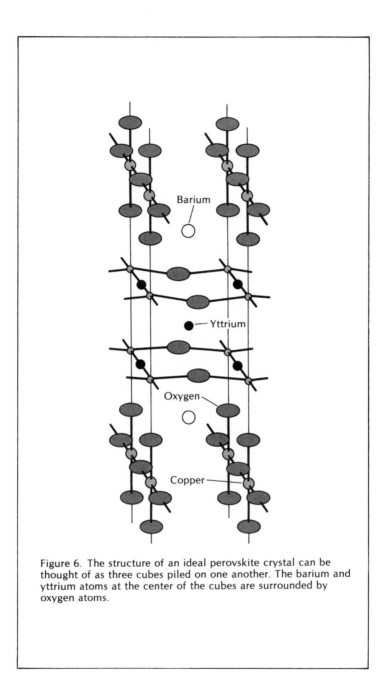

Figure 6. The structure of an ideal perovskite crystal can be thought of as three cubes piled on one another. The barium and yttrium atoms at the center of the cubes are surrounded by oxygen atoms.

entists, however, are trying very hard not to abandon it completely. They are trying to build on its obvious success with conventional superconductors while looking for ways that it must be changed to accommodate new phenomena. The important question is, what property of the ceramic could possibly create an attraction between pairs of electrons?

Some scientists have postulated that when electrons flow along the long chains that make up the oxide, there is a strong lattice interaction between oxygen atoms and the moving electrons. This interaction, they claim, produces a distortion of electric charge which in turn attracts another electron. Electron pairs are then formed, and the material becomes superconducting.

Others feel that the key lies in the surprising number of flaws that have recently been discovered in the crystal structure of high-temperature superconductors. Scientists have taken extraordinary photographs that actually show the individual atoms of these oxides. The atoms are generally piled neatly on each other like rows of marbles, but mixed into the pattern of atoms are many interruptions and defects. Scientists believe that these defects somehow create special sites where electrons can couple strongly to the vibrations of the crystal lattice. Remember that this is what happens in the BCS theory. Here again we have a mechanism for possibly creating electron pairs.

A clear understanding of why these metallic oxides function as superconductors is still proving to be elusive. For the moment there seem to be almost as many theories of high-temperature superconductors as there are solid-state physicists.

MATERIALS THAT GO AWAY

Compounding the difficulty faced by many scientists trying to explain high-temperature superconductivity is the phenomenon of "materials that go away," that is, the failure of one laboratory to confirm reports of superconductivity reported by another laboratory. Superconductivity often seems to exist for brief periods, which can be alternately exciting and frustrating for discoverers.

The frantic pace of research nevertheless goes on. In February of 1988, Paul Chu and his colleagues at the University of Houston identified a new material, a compound of bismuth, strontium, calcium, oxygen, and aluminum that is superconducting at temperatures up to 120K. They claim that this material, a distant cousin of the 1-2-3 oxide, has the potential of being dramatically cheaper and easier to work with than the other known high-temperature superconductors. An apparently similar material was reported by a team working at the National Research Institute for Metals in Japan. However, there are still major problems to be overcome. Fabricating the material seems to be difficult, and it seems to lose its superconductivity when carrying fairly large currents.

Meanwhile, a fourth material, containing thallium, barium, calcium, copper, and oxygen, has been discovered by a team at the University of Arkansas. Although very little is known about the role of thallium in the oxide, a group of IBM scientists confirmed in March 1988 that the material was a superconductor with a transition temperature of 125K.

As the number of different elements found to participate in superconductivity increases, many scientists are beginning to feel that one will have to put the entire periodic table together to make room-temperature superconductors.

7

TECHNOLOGIES OF
THE FUTURE

Imagine going into a hardware store to buy some wire and being asked if you wanted the regular or the superconducting kind. Until several years ago, this would have been considered a laughable question, straight out of the latest science-fiction magazine. Today, there are serious scientists who are beginning to think that the possibility of such an encounter is not that remote.

Finding a superconductor that requires no cooling is still a long way off. But for many applications a superconductor at liquid-nitrogen temperatures is good enough. Scientists are very fond of repeating that liquid nitrogen costs as much as milk.

High-temperature superconductivity could affect the quality of our everyday life in countless ways. Superconducting transmission lines, for example, would make it possible to eliminate much of the huge amount of the world's electrical energy now lost to resistance. Not having to worry about transmission losses means that power plants, both conventional and nuclear, could be located in remote areas, far enough from people to ease their concerns of danger and pollution. One can envision levitating cars as well as trains. Supercomputers would be free of the enormous amount of heat they generate and could be made more compact. Superpowerful magnets might make the difference between failure and success in the nuclear fusion program. One of the benefits of fusion would be an almost unlimited supply of cheap electricity.

The economic implications are also vast and difficult to predict. Industry, both here and abroad, is beginning to invest large amounts of money in superconducting research. The U.S. government is also beginning to enter the contest. A recent federal study estimated that superconductivity would be at least a $15 billion business by the year 2000. The Department of Energy is redirecting money into high-temperature superconductivity, as is the National Science Foundation. In the Congress, a House Task Force on High Technology and Competitiveness sponsored a conference entitled "Breakthrough in Superconductivity: The Race to Commercialize."

As expected, there are still many hurdles to overcome. Not the least of these are the legal problems involving patents. Not only have various researchers applied for patents on each new material that is developed by them, but IBM and Bell Labs are both trying to patent the entire class of high-temperature superconductors. Given the slow pace of such confrontations, it should take years to find our way through the legal maze.

The major hurdles, of course, are the technical challenges that must be overcome before the new superconductors can be fully exploited. What is the best way to turn these brittle ceramics into useful wires and ribbons for large-scale applications? How high a current can the superconducting wires carry before losing their superconducting properties? These questions must be answered, and research continues at an intense pace. In laboratories on three continents, scientists are mixing and brewing chemicals in ways that remind one of the ancient alchemists. Their hope is not only to create a superconductor at even higher temperatures, but to overcome some of the key technical challenges that stand in the way of turning these materials into useful products for society (see Table 3).

TABLE 3. POTENTIAL SUPERCONDUCTOR APPLICATIONS

Use	Description	Time Frame
	ELECTRONICS	
Computer Interconnections	Superconductors to wire one chip to another inside a computer; could speed up computers.	Less than five years
SQUIDS	Extremely sensitive magnetic sensors for detecting brain signals, underground minerals, and submarines.	Less than five years
Computers and computer chips	Extremely fast yet small computers.	Long-term
	ELECTRIC POWER AND MAGNETIC APPLICATIONS	
Electric Power Transmission	Superconducting power lines to transmit electricity without loss of power.	Long-term
Energy Storage	Electric energy stored indefinitely as a circulating current. Could be used by utilities to provide electricity at peak times or by military to provide energy for large lasers.	Long-term
Motors and Generators	Smaller and lighter motors or generators for use on ships and submarines.	Long-term
Magnetic Levitation	Trains magnetically levitated above the rails, allowing trains to travel swiftly and smoothly.	Long-term
Magnetic Separation	Powerful magnets for separating steel scrap, purifying ore streams and desulfurizing coal.	Over 10 years.

Source: Office of Technology Assessment.

69

SUPERCONDUCTING MAGNETS

Electromagnets have become an essential component in almost every area of our technological life. They are integral parts of the generators that make our electricity and of motors that lift and move vast quantities of materials across the world. They are found in simple hand tools and in complex diagnostic equipment such as the magnetic-resonance imaging devices.

Electromagnets are usually made by winding an iron core with many layers and turns of copper wire. When electric current is passed through the wire, a magnetic field is produced. The function of the core is to increase the strength of the magnet. It does this by becoming a magnet itself and adding its field to the one produced by the coils of wire. But iron cores are heavy, and large electromagnets are massive and bulky—hardly something to move about easily.

A superconducting magnet could achieve the same magnetic field as one of these large electromagnets without the use of a core. Without a core, it would be smaller and more mobile. When used aboard an airplane or rocket, for example, it could greatly increase the payload, saving thousands of dollars per flight.

A powerful conventional electromagnet, like the one at Brookhaven National Laboratory that is used for nuclear accelerators, can consume as much electricity as is generated by a small power station. Because it uses standard copper wire, tremendous quantities of heat are produced. Hundreds of gallons of water must be pumped through the magnet each minute to keep it from melting. A superconducting magnet could eliminate a large part of this expensive and complex system needed to service conventional magnets, as well as reducing electric costs.

Many of the magnets used in scientific work already use superconductors. And scientists in the United States are planning to use superconductors in the construction

The tunnel of the main particle accelerator at Fermilab in Batavia, Illinois. Particle accelerators use giant arrays of magnets to focus and accelerate particle beams. The lowermost group of magnets (arrow) are super-conducting and comprise the Tevatron, the most powerful accelerator in the world today.

of the world's largest and most powerful particle accelerator, called the *Superconducting Super Collider (SSC)*. It will have a circumference of 82.9 kilometers (about 52 miles). Approximately 10,000 massive and expensive superconducting magnets will be placed around the circumference to focus and accelerate the particle beams that will break matter into its most fundamental constituents. To do the same job with conventional magnets would come close to exceeding the budget of the United States.

SQUIDS

Another superconducting device of great value and interest doesn't make big magnetic fields, but rather is very sensitive to the presence of small magnetic fields. It is called a SQUID, which is an acronym for *S*uperconducting *Qu*antum *I*nterference *D*evice. SQUIDs can detect magnetic fields less than ten-billionths that of the earth.

Physicists use SQUIDs to search for gravitational waves and many other physical phenomena that produce small changes in magnetic fields. The gravitational waves are predicted by Einstein's general theory of gravitation but have yet to be observed.

Geologists use SQUIDs to prospect for oil and mineral deposits. These deposits distort the earth's local magnetic field and can therefore be detected with a sensitive instrument such as a SQUID. Scientists often carry their SQUIDs on airplanes and helicopters for quick surveys of certain terrains.

Today's SQUIDs use liquid helium, which requires bulky insulation and makes them difficult to transport. The use of high-temperature superconductors, operating with liquid nitrogen, would require less insulation and make the device much more portable.

A relatively new instrument, called a *magnetoencephalograph,* has recently been developed to study the functioning of the brain. It uses probes made of SQUIDs

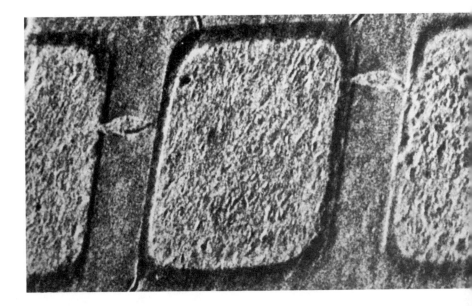

*The first high-temperature superconducting
quantum interference device (SQUID), magnified
over 500 times. SQUIDs are used by
physicists, geologists, and medical diagnosticians
to detect minute magnetic fields.*

to measure brain waves. These waves consist of magnetic fields that are produced by the electrical activity of
the nerve cells in the brain. It can also detect the faint
magnetic signals associated with the electrical activity of
the heart.

Here again, the bulky insulation required with brain
superconductors often makes it difficult to get close to a
patient. Getting close is important because the sensitiv-
ity of many of the probes used in magnetoencephalog-
raphy decreases very fast with increasing distance. The
use of liquid nitrogen would certainly help solve this
problem since less insulation would be required for the
superconducting probes.

73

MAGNETIC RESONANCE IMAGING

In medicine, superconductors form the basis of the *magnetic resonance imaging (MRI)* machine, one of the most exciting developments of the past decade. The MRI is used in hospitals as an important tool to diagnose medical disorders. The patient is first placed inside a magnet large enough to accommodate a human body. Radio waves are then used to probe the chemical makeup of tissue inside the body. Doctors can use the beautifully detailed images that are generated to diagnose a brain tumor, for example, without worrying about the tissue damage caused by X rays.

This can be done with conventional magnets, and in fact there is much research in new permanent-magnet materials. But the cost is still prohibitively high, placing an enormous economic burden on hospitals. Even with superconducting magnets, MRI machines can be very expensive. MRI has proven to be such a valuable medical diagnostic tool that its use is nevertheless spreading fast, even though the annual cost of just the helium, the coolant used in the superconducting MRI machines, can be as high as $35,000. In addition, there is also the cost of operating the paraphernalia of liquid-helium refrigeration.

MRIs are also physically very large so that they use a great deal of valuable hospital space. Their space requirement is, to a large extent, due to the need for all the additional equipment needed to minimize the loss of

An array of superconducting sensors mounted within a large thermally insulated container is used to record the magnetic field produced by brain activity near the scalp.

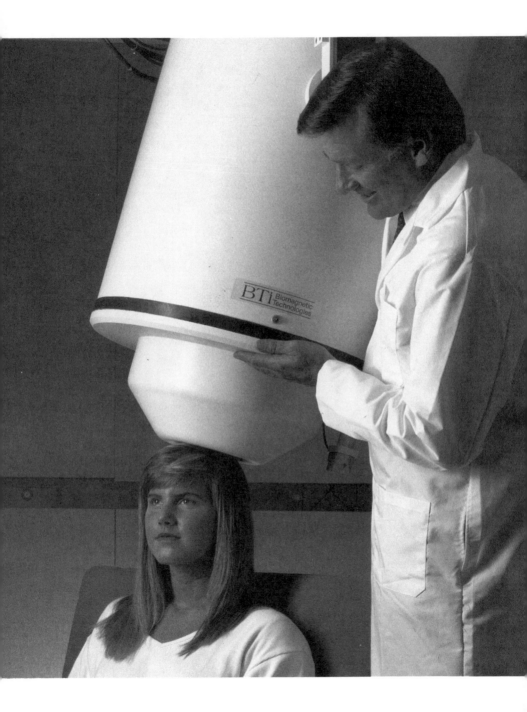

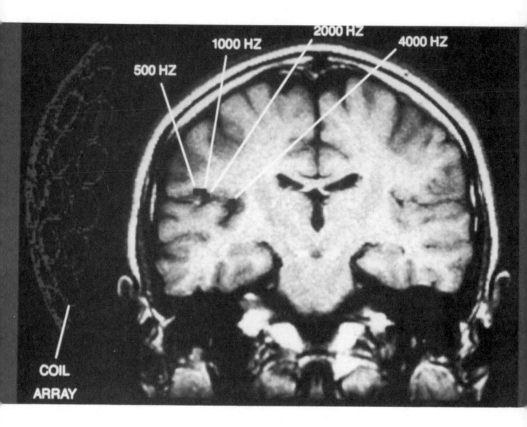

500 HZ   1000 HZ   2000 HZ   4000 HZ

COIL
ARRAY

Magnetic resonance imaging (MRI) uses radio waves and magnetic fields to probe the brain and other parts of the body. This particular image shows the location of brain activity in response to tones of the indicated frequencies, measured in hertz (Hz).

helium. There is always the inevitable thick insulation, but many machines also have complicated helium-recycling vapor-recovery systems to preserve the liquid helium.

If liquid nitrogen could be used, much of this bulk could be abandoned. High-temperature superconductors could produce smaller, less expensive, and probably more powerful machines. These improvements would certainly bring a large increase in the number of MRIs available to medical institutions.

SUPERCONDUCTING COMPUTERS

Superconductors could be one of the major factors in the evolution of the next generation of computers. If the connections between all the internal parts of a computer could be made superconducting, there would be a dramatic increase in the speed with which computers function. There would be less heat generated so that computers could be made smaller and more compact. Computers require a great deal of space for cooling devices that eliminate the heat generated by their circuits.

The speed with which a computer operates is also limited by the time it takes for its switches to operate. Superconductors are already being used to create super-fast switches called *Josephson junctions.* These switches are named for Brian Josephson, a British physicist working at Cambridge University who shared the Nobel Prize in physics for 1973 for predicting the behavior on which they are based.

Josephson junctions consist of a thin layer of insulating material sandwiched between layers of a superconducting material. They require incredibly little power to operate as a switch. This low power consumption produces less heat, again leading to more compact computers.

IBM spent more than twenty years developing Josephson junctions in their attempt to build a supercomputer. They abandoned their effort for both technical and economic reasons. Japanese companies have continued the work, however, and are hopeful that eventually high-temperature materials can be used to fabricate the switch. Supercomputers 1,000 times faster than those now being produced would then be possible.

MAGNETIC LEVITATION

Certainly, one of the most widely heralded benefits of superconductivity in the popular press has been the *maglev,* or *magnetically levitated* superconducting train. It is a startling idea. Trains without wheels and friction, floating silently above the tracks, supported by a magnetic field. But such trains already exist.

The idea of the maglev, first proposed in the 1960s, is that electromagnets attached to the moving train would induce magnetic fields in their guideways or tracks that would support, or levitate, the train. A system based on this principle and called the "Transrapid" has been developed in Germany. It uses conventional electromagnets and can propel trains along with speeds up to 250 miles (400 km) per hour. The Japanese National Railway has developed a system that uses low-temperature superconducting magnets, which they claim is more stable than the German one.

Scientists at Japan's Mercantile Marine University in Kobe have been working on a prototype of a ship whose propulsion system is based on a similar principle. The magnetic force propelling the ship forward is generated by a superconducting magnet on board the ship and an electric current generated in the seawater.

Scientists expect that since more powerful magnetic fields can be produced by using high-temperature su-

The Japanese "maglev" (magnetic levitation)
train uses superconductors to float silently
and swiftly above the tracks.

*Manufacture of a Japanese ship with a
propulsion system that uses superconducting
electromagnets. It rides the waves by the
intake and expulsion of ocean water.*

perconductors in these devices, they will be more reliable and efficient.

SUPERCONDUCTING DREAMS

Scientists have projected large-scale superconducting generators that promise to be more reliable and cheaper to operate than conventional generators. A large generator without an iron core is much easier to handle since it is much lighter. In electric generators, mechanical power rotates a magnet, which induces an electric current in a coil surrounding the magnet. There are predictions that if the field were generated by a superconducting electromagnet, the electrical output could be doubled.

Utility companies are beginning to conceive of large underground loops of superconducting cable that could store huge amounts of electrical energy for future use. This has more advantages for immediate development than the use of superconducting transmission lines. Less wire is required, and cooling with liquid nitrogen is feasible. A full-scale *superconducting magnetic storage unit (SMES)* has actually been designed. It is estimated that it will cost $1 billion. The Los Alamos National Laboratory, in New Mexico, actually built and operated a small version of SMES cooled with liquid helium. It is hoped that these small units will be able to store the energy produced by small and erratic sources such as solar cells and windmills.

Although a practical electric automobile is still a long way off, engineers at the Ford Motor Company are beginning to devote serious thought to the development of such a vehicle as the possibility of superconductors at room temperature looms.

Electric companies are beginning to ponder the possibility of using superconductors to transmit and distribute electric power. As mentioned earlier, there are tremendous losses of electrical energy in the form of heat due to electrical resistance. Supercomputing transmission wires would eliminate much of this loss.

But the all-important economic benefit of the use of superconductors would be in refrigeration. By making refrigeration systems less complex, superconductors would greatly reduce the cost of refrigeration.

MATERIAL PROBLEMS

One of the major problems facing the use of high-temperature products is how to transform a hard, brittle ceramic into wire, tape, and thin films. The ceramic is also known to lack mechanical strength. It will not, for example, easily withstand the mechanical stresses that usually act on the winding of a large electromagnet.

Another serious obstacle is that these ceramics have low critical currents. The material will simply not carry large amounts of electric current without losing its superconducting properties.

But some progress is being made. IBM recently announced that large amounts of current had been measured in a specially prepared thin film. The density of current carried was roughly 1,000 times the density carried in ordinary household wiring. Scientists speak of "current density" in these applications because the superconducting material is usually so thin. An electric current of milliamps (thousandths of an ampere) in a thin wire can translate to many amperes in a thick wire. The films produced by IBM are one-hundredth the diameter of a human hair.

Such films are used in SQUIDs. They are also used in electronic circuits, where they make up the electric wires on the surfaces of computer chips. Scientists at IBM felt that the process could eventually be used in electric transmission lines and electromagnets.

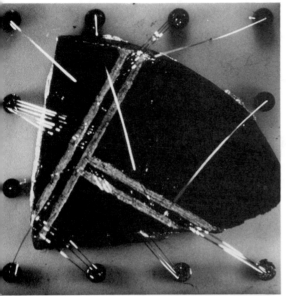

Left: Scientists at IBM developed this high-temperature superconducting thin film mounted on a substrate. It was used to demonstrate for the first time that such films could carry large amounts of current. Below: An electron-beam vapor deposition system used to prepare superconductor thin films. Electron beams heat the component materials (yttrium, barium, and copper), which are deposited as a thin film one-millionth of a meter thick onto a substrate.

The future of high-temperature superconductivity promises to be as exciting as the past. It is impossible to predict whether these wonderful new materials will ever become practical and economical. Much has yet to be done to learn how to adapt the production techniques of research laboratories to the practical manufacturing needs of large-scale industry. If the history of science gives us any hint about the future of superconductors, it is probably that one day we may well find them being used in ways we can't imagine today.

GLOSSARY

absolute zero The theoretical limit to how cold any given system can be. It is at this point that all atomic and molecular motion ceases.

atom The smallest unit of any pure substance. All matter is made up of different kinds of atoms. An atom itself is made up of smaller particles, such as neutrons, protons, and electrons.

barium An element whose properties are similar to those of calcium.

BCS theory A theory that explains superconductivity in terms of bound electron pairs that are formed by the interaction of the electrons with a metal lattice.

ceramic An earthenware product made by firing clay. A ceramic is usually a poor conductor of electricity.

Cooper pair A pair of electrons that somehow experience an attractive force and are coupled together. They are central to the BCS theory and are thought

to be the carriers of electric current in a superconductor.

critical magnetic field, B(c) The strength of the magnetic
field at which superconductivity completely disappears.

critical temperature, T(c) The temperature below which
certain elements become superconducting.

Dewar flask A double-walled evacuated flask, similar to
the common Thermos bottle, used to hold cold liquids.

electrical resistance During the flow of electricity
through a conductor, the loss of electrical energy
caused by the collision of electrons with lattice atoms.

gadolinium An element that, along with iron, chromium,
and cerium, forms paramagnetic salts and is used
for magnetic cooling.

helium The second lightest element, normally a gas at
room temperatures. It is extremely unreactive.

helium I Liquid helium above a temperature of 2.17K.

helium II Liquid helium at a temperature below 2.17K,
when it becomes a superfluid.

ion An atom with either an excess or deficiency of electrons, and therefore an electric charge.

Jahn-Teller effect The theory named for Herman Jahn
and Edward Teller that predicts an interaction of
electrons with the lattice of metallic oxides.

Josephson junction A superfast switch used in many
computers. It consists of a thin layer of insulating
material sandwiched between layers of superconducting material.

Joule-Thompson effect The name given to the temperature drop that accompanies the throttling process.

Kelvin scale A temperature scale using the same degrees as the Celsius scale but with zero defined as absolute zero. Kelvin is the scale used almost universally in scientific work.

lambda point The changeover temperature of 2.17K, below which helium I is transformed into helium II.

lanthanum An active metal element whose properties resemble those of yttrium. It is a member of the so-called scandium family of elements.

maglev (magnetic levitation) Electromagnets attached to a moving train that induce magnetic fields in the tracks and support, or levitate, the train.

magnetic resonance imaging (MRI) An important tool to diagnose medical disorders that uses radio waves and magnetic fields to probe the chemical makeup of tissues inside the body.

magnetoencephalograph A new instrument that uses SQUIDs to measure brain waves.

Meissner effect The expulsion of all magnetic fields from the interior of a superconductor.

nitrogen barrier The temperature, 77K, at which the ordinary gaseous nitrogen becomes a liquid.

1-2-3 compound A superconducting ceramic with the approximate composition $YBa_2Cu_3O_7$, so called for its relative atomic proportions of yttrium, barium, and copper.

paramagnetic salts Certain elements that behave like little magnets when they interact chemically with other elements to form a crystal.

perovskites A class of ceramics that contain oxygen combined with metal elements.

rare earths A group of seventeen elements that are called rare because they were first found in rare minerals.

sintering The process of combining elements in powder form and subjecting them to high temperatures and pressures to form a solid.

strontium An element similar to barium but with a smaller atomic structure.

superconducting magnetic storage unit (SMES) A large underground loop of superconducting cable used to store large amounts of electrical energy.

superconducting quantum interference device (SQUID) A device used to detect extremely small magnetic fields.

Superconducting Super Collider (SSC) The world's largest and most powerful particle accelerator, which is being planned by the United States and to be built in Texas.

superconductivity The loss in some materials of all electrical resistance at supercold temperatures.

supercurrents Also called persistent currents, currents that circulate in electric circuits and persist long after the original energy source is removed from the circuit.

superfluid A liquid that, like helium II, has virtually no viscosity.

temperature A measure of the average energy of a system of atoms.

throttling process The temperature drop that accompanies the process in which a liquid or gas at high pressure seeps through a tiny opening into a region of low pressure.

type II superconductors A group of superconductors with large critical magnetic fields. An important member of this group is the niobium-germanium alloy Nb_3Ge.

viscosity A measure of the ease with which a liquid flows. The "stickier" the liquid, the greater the viscosity.

zero-point energy The minimum energy of a system of atoms, which the atoms can never rid themselves of. Atoms confined in a given space can never have zero energy.

FOR FURTHER READING

BOOKS

Asimov, Isaac. How Did We Find Out About Superconductivity? New York: Walker, 1988.

Hazen, Robert M. The Breakthrough: The Race for the
Superconductor. New York: Ballantine, 1989.

Mayo, Jonathan. Superconductivity: The Threshold of a
New Technology. Blue Hill Summit: TAB Books,
1988.

Prochnow, Dave. Superconductivity: Experiments in a
New Technology. Blue Hill Summit: TAB Books,
1988.

Schechter, Bruce. The Path of No Resistance: The Story
of the Worldwide Race That Led to the Revolution
in Superconductivity. New York: Simon and
Schuster, 1989.

ARTICLES

"The New Superconductors: Prospects for Applications." *Scientific American,* February 1989, pp. 61–69.

"Experimenting with a Superconductor." *Modern Electronics,* March 1988, pp. 60–65.

"Superconductivity: Hype vs. Reality." *Discover,* August 1987, pp. 23–32.

INDEX

Meissner effect, 44–46, 58

Meissner, Walther Hans, 44

Mercury, 18, 19, 40, 41, 42, 43

Metallic oxides, 56–57, 64

Müller, Karl Alexander, 9, 10, 11, 51, 55, 56–57, 62

Niobium, 44, 55–56

Nobel Prize, 10, 11, 47, 48

Ochsenfeld, Robert, 44

Oersted, Hans Christian, 42

1-2-3 compound, 58–62

Onnes, Heike Kamerlingh, 28, 31–32, 36, 37, 40, 41–42

Oxygen, 55, 56, 65

Paramagnetic salts, 29

Perovskites, 56, 62

Perpetual motion, 11, 40

Rare earths, 60

Reagan, Ronald, 15

Resistance, 39–41

Reverse flow, 34–35

Shake and bake, 12, 15, 61

Schluter, Michael, 12

Schrieffer, J. Robert, 47, 48

Sintering, 57

SQUIDS, 69, 72–73, 82

Strontium, 61, 65

Superconducting Magnetic storage unit (SMES), 81

Superconducting Super Collider (SSC), 72

Superconducting Quantum Interference Device. See SQUIDS

Superconductivity, 11–12, 37–51
definition, 9

Superconductors, 45
Type I, 41, 43
Type II, 41, 43–44, 45

Supercurrents, 41

Superfluids, 32–34

Tanaka, Shoji, 57

Technology, future, 67–84

Teller, Edward, 56

Temperatures, 19–21
lowest achieved, 21
useful, 21

Teslas, 42, 43

Tevatron, 71

Thermal energy, 38

Thermometer helium-gas, 29–30

Thermometers, 17–19

Third Law of Thermodynamics, 21

Thompson, J. J., 37

Thompson, William (Lord Kelvin), 19–20

ABOUT THE AUTHOR

Albert Stwertka holds a Ph.D. in physics, which he teaches at the United States Merchant Marine Academy in Kings Point, New York. He is also the author of numerous science books for children and young adults, many of them written in collaboration with his wife, Eve. His recent Franklin Watts titles include *Genetic Engineering* and *Recent Revolutions in Physics*. Dr. Stwertka makes his home on Long Island. He has two sons.